Julie Shields *and* Mia Logan, PhD

Thank FORWARD

A Gratitude Action Kit

REDFeather™

MIND | BODY | SPIRIT

Printed in China

Designed by Brenda McCallum
Type set in Linotype

ISBN: 978-0-7643-5864-7
Printed in China

Published by Red Feather Mind, Body, Spirit
An imprint of Schiffer Publishing, Ltd.
4880 Lower Valley Road
Atglen, PA 19310
Phone: (610) 593-1777
Fax: (610) 593-2002
E-mail: Info@schifferbooks.com
Web: www.redfeathermbs.com

I'm a big proponent of the benefits
of having an attitude of gratitude.
If you are, too, you'll love *Thank Forward.*
It's a beautiful way to express appreciation to people
in your life and then experience those good feelings
bouncing back to you and forward to others.
Join the Thank Forward movement!

—Ken Blanchard
Cofounder and chief spiritual officer
of the Ken Blanchard Companies and coauthor of
The New One-Minute Manager

*The best way to find yourself is to lose
yourself in the service of others.*

GANDHI

Acknowledgments

The birth of *Thank Forward* took several years to develop. Julie
and Mia acknowledge the following individuals with gratitude for
their mentorship, guidance, and contributions: Tammy Totoro-
Dick (our beautiful and gifted artist), Carol Franco, Linda Logan-
Condon, Art Logan-Condon, Shari L. Cordova, Wifrid R. Koponen,
Dinah Roseberry, Carey Massimini, Pete Schiffer, and our friends
and family.

Dedication

We dedicate this gratitude action kit
to all the recipients of these acts of kindness.
May they bring you joy and comfort.

Contents

Introduction

Within the blueprint of your heart lies a buried treasure. This treasure is much bigger than words or tangible objects, so glorious and abundant that once you open it, your entire being will fill with a magnetic radiance. The treasure is felt through your body, thoughts, and interactions with others. Rainy days become sunny, heavy shoulders float like a feather, and rocky roads lead to fields of gold. We are all born with this hidden treasure. Most importantly, we are all capable of using the treasure at any moment. The treasure is happiness, and the key to opening it is gratitude.

Gratitude is the secret sauce to *feeling* happiness. Gratitude stimulates dopamine, which increases activity and makes social interactions more enjoyable. Cultivating gratitude boosts serotonin and, ultimately, forces you to focus more on positive aspects of your life. The best part about it is that gratitude is unlimited; the more of it you consume, the more you have left over!

Gratitude is about the future, not the past. When people cooperate with others, gratitude changes what you value. It pushes people to work in the moment to benefit what is to come. In doing so, it is an extremely active state. It will influence what you do next. We encourage you to take action and THANK FORWARD. Here are our stories on how we took action.

Julie's Story

I felt as though I was ready to give up. I wanted to run away and start a new life over in some dusty little town that fell off the map. I've been working since I was fourteen years old and started a corporate career while I was in college. After graduating from college, I attempted to fill the mold of what I thought was the American Dream—becoming a career woman, a wife, and a mother, with lots of friends who were living the same American Dream.

The real story is that I had a few pregnancies that ended in miscarriage, went through a divorce, and worked in a career that left me unfulfilled. After years of hiding my disappointments, I had to face the truth: I was burned out, and my physical health and stamina suffered. I attempted to find something to blame for what I had become—overweight and unhealthy. I admit I made poor choices in relationships but found my way out and above them. I was unhappy, and there is no miracle pill to cure what I was suffering from. I took all of this out on my body, mind, and spirit. What I needed was a major change in attitude.

As I was hitting the bottom of the pit of my self-loathing, I came across *Hay House Radio* on the internet. I had a few inspirational books on my shelf, collecting dust, and realized some of the authors had their own radio shows. I've always believed in signs and universal messages. I hoped I would catch a glimmer of something from this inspirational material to get me out of my funk. From the moment I learned about *Hay House Radio*, I was hooked. I listened while working, taking daily walks, and at home while doing chores. I must've listened to a half-dozen radio shows the first week. Sure enough, the message came through loud and clear—not from just one author or radio host but from all of them. I can sum up the message in one sentence: "The secret to happiness is gratitude!"

Gratitude? That seems easy. I sat on my deck in the clear, fresh Colorado air and jotted down a list of things that I was grateful for. It was amazing how quickly the list grew into several pages. I could not keep this wonderful feeling to myself, so I began expressing my gratitude to those on my list. Just a quick text or comment in a conversation to say, "Hey, I love you and am grateful that you are part of my life." The responses I received were so genuine and bright, I felt pure joy in my heart. Not only was I feeling better, my loved ones were lighting up. Imagine what this feeling would do for strangers.

When it came to sharing this joy with strangers, I felt cautious—outside my comfort zone. I wanted to be genuine, but I didn't want to make anyone uncomfortable. I didn't want or expect anything in return. As an experiment, whenever I went to a restaurant drive-thru, I would pay for the person's order behind me. This was safe, as I didn't need to make any human interaction; the cashier would do it for me, and I could do it quickly. The first few times I did this, I drove off as fast as I could so that no one could catch up to me and give me a weird look. I would giggle from the joy of it. Then it happened to me—twice in one week! The person in front of me paid for my drive-thru order. WOW! This was truly contagious.

If this works in a drive-thru, what other selfless act of kindness could I do to make someone's day brighter?

This is where my personal Thank Forward movement was born. Everyday acts of kindness that cost little to no money and time, yet have the ability to make someone smile. I am so grateful I am able to give and accept joy. My dream is to inspire others to join me and create a social movement of "Thanking Forward."

Mia's Story

For fifteen years, I have been go, go, go. I have always been a driver sort of person. I pushed the limit and took on new challenges. In 2003, I decided to go back to school and get my PhD.

I went all out. The PhD program was a lot more work than I'd expected. I did the work and completed my dissertation in four years. This just about killed me. During this time, I owned my own consulting business. I finished the PhD in 2007. In the fall of 2008, the market crashed, and my business closed after thirteen years. I was devastated.

I tapped my imagination to look for ways to make a living. I sold things on eBay and created classes to help doctoral students. I coached them and edited their dissertations and papers. I lived on a tight budget. I got rid of my home phone, dropped cable television, and disconnected my internet service. I deferred my student loans. I went to soup kitchens and used food stamps. I had to file for bankruptcy. I was able to save my house, and I was grateful for that. It was humiliating. I reached a low in my life and suffered from despair. Depression runs in my family. I was in its grip, and I had to figure out how to climb out of it.

It took me a year and a half to land a full-time job. A colleague had a position and encouraged me to apply. I got the job, but I was laid off ten months later. I had been starting to pull myself out again, and then at Christmastime, I had to find another job. From my network, I was able to land another full-time job. That job was not something I wanted. I really wanted my business back again, but the market had not fully recovered from the 2008 crash, so I chose to stay in this job for seven years. It was highly stressful, and I was exhausted.

I realized four years into that job that I needed to start to take better care of myself. No one was going to do it for me. I was so fatigued and stressed. I could barely get up each morning. All I wanted to do was sleep. My MD referred me to a naturopath. I had to fill out a twenty-seven-page intake package, provide a DNA sample, and supply saliva, urine, feces, and blood for tests. I was on the verge of an autoimmune disease called leaky gut. I had chronic fatigue and adrenal fatigue. I'd suffered from chronic fatigue for the past ten to fifteen years, and I was now in stage 3.

This was my wake-up call or aha moment.

I had to make some changes in my life. This would require self-care and patience. Plus, there were things I needed to do that I did not want to do. Some of these changes were going to be major life changes! For three years now, I have had to entirely eliminate my consumption of gluten, caffeine, sugar, dairy, and alcohol. All I can drink is water. I had to get eight hours of sleep each night. The first six months, no exercise. Then, I had to walk and do yoga and nothing more. I had to take Epsom salt and magnesium baths. I had to sit in an infrared sauna three times per week. I took handfuls of herbs and vitamins and did multiple cleanses.

I had to be disciplined about these monumental changes in my life. I realized that I had to make some shifts, for my life HAD to be different. I am starting to feel better physically, but I still have a year or two to go. I have had to protect myself and create boundaries. My life is on the line!

I am grateful that I have this chance to make a change. It is time to reset and reprogram my life so I can be healthy. I learned to be patient with myself. I learned how to be kind to myself. This is a crucial part of this "Thank Forward" movement.

JOIN US.
Gratitude is all we have.
Take Action!

Instructions

Welcome to *Thank Forward*, an action-oriented kit that contains twenty-one simple, humble, and modest acts of kindness designed to ignite a fire of glorious joy in your mind, body, spirit, AND help others find joy in their lives.

Each act of kindness can be as big or as small as you wish. The point is not to spend a lot of money or time, but to take an action and live the experience with gratitude. Different suggestions and options are provided on the cards and in this book to allow for you to set your own level of comfort in your participation. Go bold, or go with simplicity. No matter what you choose, it's your actions that will create joy.

You may complete the acts on your own timeline and in any order you please. However, it is suggested to complete a minimum of three a week (over a period of seven weeks) to keep the momentum going. Some acts may take a little more time than others. It is okay to deploy them out of order. Remember to keep the journey enJOYable.

Each card is designed to contain a brief instruction and guidelines. Refer to this companion guide for additional ideas and affirmation. Follow the directions below.

1. Pull a card (may be in numerical order or in any order you choose).

2. Read and reflect on the related affirmation of the card located in this companion guide.

3. Perform the act of kindness as instructed by the card (reference this companion guide for additional information on each card).

4. Share your experience and ideas on the community feed and inspire others at www.ThankForward.com.

Suggestions

Before performing the act of kindness on each card, take a few moments to meditate or reflect on its related affirmation (presented in this companion guide).

After completing the act of kindness, pass the card on to another person (perhaps the recipient of the act) to encourage another to participate. With shared participation, YOU will initiate a glorious chain of gratitude.

Record or share the experience you felt with the act of kindness in a journal, in a doodle, on social media, or with another person.

Leave a card behind for a stranger to pick up and create a social movement.

Gather your friends and have a Thank Forward party where you can choose cards, brainstorm ideas, and create action plans. Set a date to meet again and discuss your experiences. Then, share your stories at www.ThankForward.com.

Check out www.ThankForward.com for workshops, keynote presentations, and gratitude events.

In a gentle way, you can shake the world.

GANDHI

Gratitude for Human Interaction

Affirmation

Today, I get back to basics and embrace communication through verbal or face-to-face contact with cherished people in my life. The voices and natural vibration of the world around me keep me balanced and calm. I am grateful for human interaction.

Action

Unplug for the day. Disconnect from social media and electronics for as long as you can. Getting back to basics relaxes the mind and body and creates room for balance and gratitude.

Ideas for Disconnecting to Reconnect

- Communicate verbally, by paper and pen, or in person.
- Read a book or draw to calm your mind.
- Listen, dance, or sing to music.
- Reach out to someone you have not spoken to in a long time.
- Meet a friend for coffee.
- Reconnect with a family member and spend time listening to them.

Pay it FORWARD

Gratitude for Giving without Expectation

Affirmation

Today, I look for ways to give back to people I know and even people I do not know. I choose to find ways to help others, and look for ways to alleviate someone's burden, even in just a small way.

Action

Give for the sake of giving without expecting anything in return. Pay for someone behind you in a fast-food drive-thru, coffee shop, or grocery store. You can also pay it forward without using money. Consider donating your time to a nonprofit organization or charity, walk a neighbor's dog, or listen to a friend who needs support.

Ideas for Paying It Forward

- Allow yourself to go through the day without expectations.
- Look for ways to give support to someone by listening, helping, bearing witness, etc.
- Make others a priority.
- Give thanks for your ability to give.

Gratitude for Owning the Power to Make Things Happen

Affirmation

Today, I accept the power within myself to inspire action. Action of any size is powerful.

Action

Put energy toward a cause you believe in. Volunteer, donate (money, time, or personal items), initiate a donation drive, or share your belief in a cause (via word of mouth or social media). The idea is to spread awareness about something you believe in. Change begins with effort. No matter how big or small the effort required, you have the ability to make change through taking action.

Ideas to Make It Happen

- Donate blood.
- Volunteer time with a hospital, nursing home, shelter, or animal center.
- Initiate a collection drive at a school, work, church, or local grocery store.

- Bring a group of friends together to share a meal, and have each person bring some canned goods to donate to your favorite charity.

- Support a nonprofit organization by promoting it on social media.

- Donate books to a local library or school.

- Donate unused toiletries, gently used items of clothing or household goods, and canned or dried goods to a local charity or homeless shelter.

Gratitude for Positive Thoughts, Words, and Actions

Affirmation

Today, I express my thoughts and words with positivity and light. Conversations flow easily and spread joy with others.

Action

Be positive today. Reframe your thoughts and language as you go throughout your day. If you find yourself becoming negative or cynical, take a moment, do some deep belly breathing, and bring yourself back to a positive place.

Ideas for Happy Chatter

- If you find yourself in a situation revolving around gossip or negativity, reframe it with positive words and thoughts. If this is not possible, detach or withdraw from the situation. Take some time to walk or meditate.

- If you are around people who drain you, distance yourself and protect your space.

5
Love LETTERS

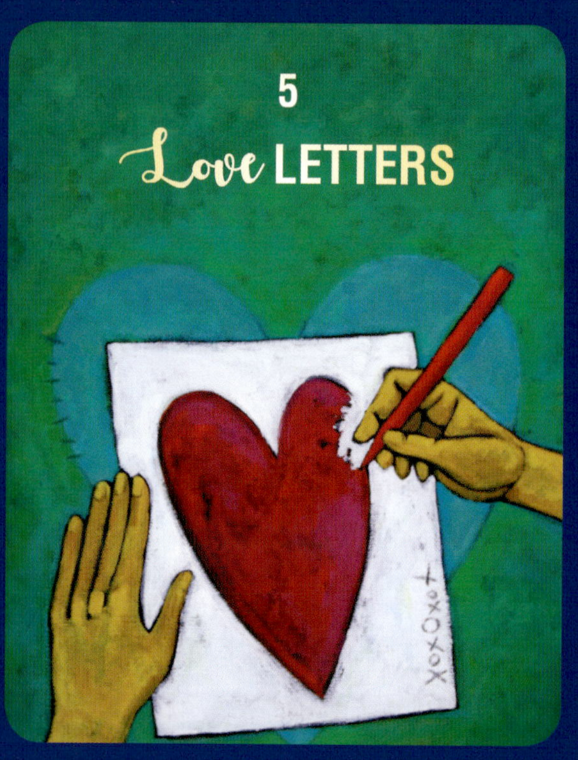

Gratitude for Expression

Affirmation

Today, I will place heartfelt feelings on paper to express my gratitude for someone else. It touches my heart to see it on paper, and I know giving this message to another person will deliver joy.

Action

Think of someone you personally know and would like to thank, perhaps someone who had an impact on you at some point in your life—a teacher, coach, friend, boss, or relative.

Ideas for Love Letters

- Give a handwritten note, a personally signed greeting card, a postcard, or a doodle that expresses your gratitude to this person.

Writing a short note, picking out a greeting card, or doodling a loving picture to someone you personally know and appreciate does not take much out of your busy day. However, these moments may make a lasting impact on you and on the receiver.

6

Love YOUR EARTH

Gratitude for Earthly Foundations

Affirmation

Today, I recognize the bounties the Earth provides and the power I have within me to protect our environment.

Action

You have the power to keep your world beautiful. Reduce, reuse, and recycle. The Earth's beauty is abundant in many ways. Take care of it, and it will care for you.

Ideas for Loving Your Earth

- Make an effort to recycle, clean up litter, bring reusable bags to the grocery store, or repurpose trash into a craft project.
- Reduce your carbon footprint. Use the bus system, walk, or bike.

Gratitude for Courage

Affirmation

Today, I say "YES" to what I desire. By saying yes to others, I often say no to the most important person in my life, ME. Today I say YES to ME.

Action

Often, when you say YES to others, you say NO to yourself. Today is the day to ask for what you really desire instead of what you believe others expect from you. Set boundaries and let go of guilt. Protect your time.

Today, you will say YES to what you want. Display your courage with your actions.

Ideas for Saying Yes to You

- Take action on an idea or desire that you've been considering, or simply say NO to something you really do not want to do.

Gratitude for Abundance

Affirmation

Today, I am grateful for warmth, shelter, health, and love.
I take a moment to recognize that my needs are fulfilled.

Action

Whether living paycheck to paycheck or beyond, living with comfort is worth more than money. If you have food, shelter, and people who love you, you are prosperous; your basic needs are provided for abundantly. Being loved is a treasure that money cannot buy. Take this card and include it with a payment or donation. With shared participation, YOU will initiate a chain of gratitude and a positive view of prosperity.

Ideas for Embracing Prosperity

- Take a moment and think about the food you eat, the roof over your head, and the people who love you. Do you have a car that allows you to travel to work or to explore the country? Is your family healthy? Do you have internet access to stay in touch with the world, to obtain access to education, and to perform work for which you are paid? Do you have clean water to drink? If you eat three meals a day, you are far better off than the one billion people on the planet who eat once a day, at most.

Gratitude for the Ability to Love Myself

Affirmation

Today, I express gratitude for the ability to love myself.
By loving myself I am able to love others with a pure heart.

Action

Today, list 100 reasons you are grateful by focusing on gratitude. Notice how your self-esteem improves.
Self-esteem holds more power than any dollar can buy.
Utilize this power to inspire others to love themselves.

Ideas for Owning It

- Take an extra challenge and list 100 things you love about yourself.

Gratitude for Generous Support and Assistance from Others

Affirmation

Today, I am especially grateful to others who give service selflessly to comfort others.

Action

Some members of our society participate in jobs to help others. Some get more recognition for their service than others. No matter what their pay level, experience, or status, such humans do these things to provide comfort and help to other humans. Take a moment to applaud the service of all who give: custodians, nurses, medical staff, people who serve you in restaurants or stores, police officers, firefighters, members of the military, teachers, housekeepers, cashiers, trash collectors, postal carriers, and others.

Ideas to Applaud Service

- Take this card and write a loving note for someone who provides selfless service. Ask the person to pass along the card in the same manner. With shared participation, YOU will initiate a glorious chain of gratitude.

Gratitude for Sharing Culture, History, and Ideas

Affirmation

Today, I take a moment to appreciate the gift of storytelling. With storytelling, we have history and the tools for growth and learning. Stories also take me away to new places and relax my mind and body.

Action

Stories are the basis for knowledge. Stories provide history, learning, and imagination. What began as oral tradition has been passed from generation to generation. Share your appreciation for the gift of stories by giving a new or used book to someone you love, reading a story to another, donating books to a charity, telling a story of your own to someone, or recommending a book to another. Share what inspires you, and be a catalyst for inspiring others.

Ideas for the Gift of Storytelling

- Give someone a copy of your favorite book, whether it be new or from your personal collection.
- Inscribe a note on the inside cover as an added bonus.

- Send a reading suggestion to someone or post it on social media. Explain what the book means to you and why you are sharing the suggestion.

- Initiate a book drive for donating to a favorite charity or cause.

- Donate new or used books to a library, hospital, shelter, or school.

- Read a book or share a story of your own with someone you love or a patient or resident of a care facility.

- Join a dog/cat shelter's reading program where you spend time with the animals and read to them.

12
Mantra MAGIC

Gratitude for an Open Heart

Affirmation

Today, I will utilize a mantra as a reminder of where I need to focus my thoughts on gratitude. This provides me with an opportunity to be grateful as I add a gratitude prayer throughout the day.

Action

Create a mantra that is simple and easy to remember. Use a Post-it note to place it on your mirror in your bathroom, in your car, on your refrigerator, or at work. Recite it and focus in on what the words mean to you.

Suggestions for Gratitude Mantras

- I experience gratitude for everything I have in my life.
- I am grateful for excellent health, prosperity, and true love.
- My life is filled with an abundance of goodness.
- All challenges are an opportunity for growth, and I am thankful for the chance to evolve.

- I am so grateful for supportive friends and a loving family.
- I appreciate everything I have in my life and always keep the door open for more blessings.
- The universe supports me and all my desires.
- I am the co-creator of my reality.
- I see the beauty in nature that surrounds me.
- I see animals as sacred and appreciate the gifts they give.
- I give thanks for the helpful spirits and ancestors that guide me in this life journey.
- I am blessed.
- I love myself unconditionally right now.

13
Lend an
INTENTIONAL SMILE

Gratitude for Lighting Up the World with Your Beautiful Face

Affirmation

Today, I will take moments to smile at strangers, friends, family, animals, and nature. As I light up my face, others will follow, and soon many hearts will feel the kindness that started with a simple gesture.

Action

Smiling is contagious. Take a moment to smile as you are reading this companion guide. How do you feel inside? Now try to frown. Notice any difference? Smiling is an act that takes little effort yet makes a BIG impact on others and on us.

Ideas for Lending an Intentional Smile

- Be intentionally kind to another person today through the expression on your face.
- Talk to someone you see often but don't visit with (maybe a neighbor or a coworker), just say "hello," sincerely compliment a stranger, or let someone go before you in line.
- Be kind, and keep smiling!

Gratitude for Pampering

Affirmation

Today, I will take a few extra moments to care for me beyond my standard routine. I love who I am, and I will be extra kind to myself.

Action

Often, we focus on others and neglect ourselves. When was the last time you scheduled time on the calendar for yourself? Stop to appreciate how your sense of humor cheers others, but also yourself. When someone thanks you for something, allow an extra moment to let the compliment really sink in. Focus on pampering yourself so you can be your best you for everyone else.

Ideas for Happy YOU Day:

- Get in touch with yourself above and beyond the activities of your daily routine. Take a bath, exercise, get a massage, journal, meditate, color in a coloring book to relax, or just pause to notice with appreciation the ways in which your mind and spirit operate. The idea is to do something nice for yourself that you don't normally do.

Gratitude for Plenty

Affirmation

Today, I am grateful for the abundance of food and nutrients available to me. I express my gratitude by sharing the abundance with another.

Action

Break bread with another and share nourishment with not only your body but also your heart.

Ideas for Breaking Bread

- Share a meal.
- Provide lunch to someone who is going through a difficult time.
- Give a fast-food gift card to a person in need.
- Drop off a bag of groceries at a local shelter.
- Drop off pet food at a humane shelter.
- Volunteer at a local shelter or food bank.

Gratitude for Positive Energy

Affirmation

Today, I recognize the greatness in others. As I go an extra step in spreading positive vibes, so will others. *Good + Good = Greatness.*

Action

A compliment can take many forms. It can be verbal, written, or doodled. It can also be given in the form of a handshake, nod, wink, or smile. Being nice is easy. The emotion it evokes is amazing. Let's spread good vibes wherever we go.

Ideas for Good Karma

- Compliment people.
- Acknowledge people by thanking them.
- Send a letter of commendation to a company you like.
- Fill out a compliment card with well-earned praise.
- Give a recommendation on social media.

17
Embody
MINDFUL EATING

Gratitude for Nourishment

Affirmation

Today, as I savor the fruits of Mother Nature, I am reminded that my body is part of nature. Eating foods that are good for my body expresses gratitude to Mother Nature and respect for myself.

Action

Mindful eating is a practice that incorporates thoughts with food. Consider where the food came from, what it took to make it, and all the efforts involved by humans and the Earth to bring nutrition to you.

By taking time to appreciate your food, you will also tend to make wiser nutritional choices.

Ideas for Embracing Mindful Eating

- Before you eat each meal today, take a moment of silence to consider where it came from, what it took to produce, and how much effort was involved. Savor each bite and acknowledge how your body feels with gratitude.

- If you are feeling especially creative, prepare a colorful meal full of natural foods and share it with others.

Gratitude for Air, Flora, Soil, and Water

Affirmation

Today, I go outside and become one with nature. I enact my senses and appreciate the sights, sounds, and smells around me. Plants bring clean air, bees pollinate flowers, and weather brings beauty in many different measures.

Action

Get in touch with nature today. Give intentional gratitude to all the nature that surrounds you.

Ideas for Hugging Mother Nature

- Even if it is cold outside, bundle up and enjoy being outdoors for a few minutes. Fresh air does wonders for the mind, body, and soul.

- Take a walk, hike, meditate in the park, breathe in fresh air, help an animal, plant a seed, or give a potted plant to a loved one.

Gratitude for Accepting Others Just as They Are

Affirmation

Today, I express my gratitude for time. By taking extra moments to slow down today, I cherish time and patience. I allow other people to have autonomy over their lives, their beliefs, and their choices.

Action

What may seem like an eternity may actually be mere seconds. Rushing may save a few moments, but the feeling of ease is worth more than the rush. When you are tempted to contradict or argue with others, pause to let them hold their own point of view. Take a moment to pause and allow a person to pass you through a door or in a traffic lane.

Ideas for Acting with Patience

- Make an intentional effort to hold the door open.
- Allow a car to merge ahead.
- Allow someone ahead of you in line.
- Offer a paper towel to another in the restroom.
- Listen as someone expresses a different point of view.
- Return your shopping cart to the store.

Gratitude for Unexpected Gifts

Affirmation

Today, I choose to express love in any way I am able. I take comfort in knowing that there is enough love to spread beyond the stars. The world will benefit from my loving embrace.

Action

Take an opportunity to express your love in an unexpected way; allow your happy message to be seen by anyone lucky enough to find it. There is a sense of letting go and the element of surprise when someone sees or happens upon it.

Ideas for Spreading the Love

- Write a happy message, create a doodle, or share a favorite quotation on a piece of paper. Post it in a place that will benefit others (restroom, work or neighborhood bulletin board, a trailhead, a friend or neighbor's door, etc.).

Gratitude for Being Resourceful, Resilient, and Creative

Affirmation

Today, I initiate a movement as big or as small as I desire, just because I want to.

Action

Humans have the innate ability to be resourceful, resilient, and creative. No matter how big or small, your assignment for today is to create your own gratitude movement. Humans hold the key to their own power. Your mission is to unlock it. Be an example and initiate a movement, no matter how small or large. You have the power. Today, the world is especially grateful for you!

Ideas for Creating Your Own Challenge

- 💛 If you are feeling stuck, re-create a previous challenge with your own twist or take on two of the challenges in one day.

Conclusion

Congratulations! You did it! By completing these 21 actions in this kit, you are officially the "creator of your own gratitude" movement. Close your eyes, smile, and feel your heartbeat. Do you feel the joy pumping through your senses? Keep the joy going by continuing to Thank Forward and inspire others.

Should you want to continue practicing your action and gratitude—and by all means you should!—we invite you to use the replacement cards that are available from your retailers!